I0517711

The Hobo Bob Cantos

Poems by Steven H. Bridgens

OAC
PRESS
OSAGE ARTS COMMUNITY

OAC Press
Belle, Missouri

Copyright © Steven H. Bridgens, 2024
First Edition: 1 3 5 7 9 10 8 6 4 2
ISBN: 978-1-958182-18-5
LCCN: 2022944299

Cover photo: Library of Congress
Author photo: Steven Bridgens

Acknowledgments

To All My Muses, Everyone

The author would like to thank: Prospero's Books, Spartan Press, The Osage Arts Community, Mark McClane, Tony Hayden, Jason Ryberg, Kathy Ann Tate, The Red Barn Studio, The Lester Raymer Society, Emily Howe, Marsha Howe, Will Leathem, Dr. Tanya Kelley, Dr. Patricia Cleary Miller, Jane Pearce, Mick Jagger, Keith Richards, Bruce Springsteen, Bob Dylan, Rick Chasteen, Bruce & Nancy Waugh, R. Getty, Betty Mantz, Arthur Bridgens, Geoff Oelsner, Sam Blackwell, Thom & Cecilia Lonnecker, John Daily, Sue Ellen Adair, Janet Nima Taylor, Charlie Sloan, Richard Grossinger, Paul Shepard, Barbara Werner Baxter, Gary Snyder, Naomi Schupp-Pavey.

And to those that have gone before: Virginia Scott Miner, Thomas Vibert, Bob Rausch & the Arctic Research Center, William Neale Mullins, Francis Ruth Hamilton Bridgens, Dr. James Getty Bridgens, Patricia Gray, Kate Ghio, Chris Theis, Gregory Pierson, Victor Campbell, Raymond Starsmann, Roberto Calasso, Ian Fleming, Lawrence Durrell, Marcel Duchamp, Norman O. Brown, Raymond Chandler, Edith Hamilton, Thomas Bullfinch, T. S. Eliot, William S. Burroughs, Marnie Weldon, Lois N. Adair, Gary Snyder, Jamaica Lee Rock and Dick Gregory.

With special thanks to every library & museum in the world.

Table of Contents

Dedication

...waste your summer praying in vain,
for a savior to rise from these streets.

~Bruce Springsteen, *Thunder Road*

I cannot pretend, of course, that I recall all
of these dialogues, verbatim.

~Frederic Prokosch, *The Missolonghi*
Manuscript

These poems are dedicated to those that have gone on
before and helped to clear a path.

We should be mindful of the unmarked graves along the
levee as we head down to the river, thick with the patrimony
of our forebears.

We follow the trail left by those lonely scouts too long out
on point.

They've drunk all their whisky, lost their horses, blankets
and rifles, but fight on till the very end.

~SHB

The Hobos Amongst Us

Not all in wantonness do tramps carve their monikers.
~Jack London, *The Road*

Sez I: *No matter where you go, there you are.*
Sez he: *Yeah, but better there than here.*

I
When a character emerges from the mist of creation,
it is incumbent upon the author, the creator, to *explique*
a bit about the ideas bouncing around in his head,
figuring out whence they come, and then to show
his work. Or not. Perhaps, maybe.

To put a finger on the pulse of our history,
for a minute—the phenomenon of the Hobo
emerged on the North American continent during the
heyday of the railroads, some years after the Civil War,
when times were hard and trains were slow.

Men, usually, would take to the rails, relishing the wide-
open space of the big sky country, the danger of rough
rail travel and unforgiving yard bulls.

They sought opportunity and adventure, the freedom
and liberty guaranteed to us all, or once was. Some of
us anyway, if ya got the ticket.

Before the railroad it was possible to get away to the
great unknown wilderness where the only law was
natural law: the law of the ecosystem, the food chain
and the trophic level. Eat and be eaten.

Live, eat, learn, breed, die, be eaten, decompose and
return. Nowadays it's all a bit more complicated,
as you may have noticed.

II
Perhaps the Hobos were a manifestation of the nation's
dream, of god's will, his ordained Manifest Destiny.

Or even more potently, the subtext of a subtle subconscious
realization that there are limits to everything.

We've reached the terrestrial limit of our Manifest Destiny
at the Pacific Ocean, the Santa Monica Pier, or far Catalina.

There still may be traces of it remaining in Alaska and the
Yukon. These very real and concrete boundaries tend to
increase anxiety.

Beyond our shores, Manifest Destiny transforms into
Empire pretty quickly and we live the consequences of
acts hundreds of years old every minute. Just turn on the
news. I dare you.

The only remaining unexplored territories, besides the ocean
depths and outer space, are internal: the ephemeral and
invisible realms.

Someone has now been everywhere. Just follow the trash.
We are at the end of the line and the illusion of that final
cool somewhere.

Perhaps that is why we are all so nervous.
Now: *Which way to go? Which way to go?*

Yes, well, here we are then. This is all there is, except, of course, death.

III
The 'bos went on the road, footloose and fancy-free, jumping up, grabbing on, riding the rails. We're seldom truly content in the now, unless traveling on, traveling light.

Once they got to where they thought they were heading, that's it, there they were. Nothing has really changed. Symbolically speaking, of course,

Maybe they would become as Ronin, leaderless Samurai released from service by their Lord, wandering goalless, searching for direction.

Or mendicants, seekers like Shakumani, the Buddha, looking for something, which he later discovered is only to be found inside, not out there, ever.

The idea has begun to mean something to us, finally, trapped in what has become the norm of our global life since the Big One: the rat trap of the Matrix, the Big Machine, extruding everything we think we need.

Then finally, pressured by oneself to either jump ship or *blow a fifty amp fuse*. No more workin' the levee camps for the man, not for one more minute.

Always leap, but always look. Plan your escape. This grasp of new freedom can be represented by the Hobo, perhaps just some poor guy forced into an escape by circumstances.

IV

He's a true minimalist, owning little, carrying less in his
man-purse, in a bindle tied onto a staff, sleeping rough
under the stars beside the tracks.

He was forced out of the cage by unknown pressures,
now a wandering medium-sized mammal again, following
the seasons: the elk, buffalo, the parallel rails, wherever
they lead.

Like in the past, the migrants turn North in the spring,
back South in the fall. Railroads generally head East
to West and back again. They meet in the Midwest at
a crossroads somewhere big trucks park..

V

Hobos evolved their own symbolic language, and their
version of the goalless goal. Such is life, actually, no
matter what they taught you in school. Unlearn it now,
before it's too late.

The *Hobo americanus* and his global antecedents are
archetypes of the subconscious, our shadow self,
the *doppelgänger* that's always out there.

His is the face in the mirror asking every morning:
What are you doing with your life? and *Why bother?*

He sometimes catches you musing, looking out a dusty
window at his reflection, tapping your pencil in lieu of
action.

Hatch a plan for your own big red freight car to finally
roll out of Dodge, out of wherever you are, out of
whatever trap your poor leg is caught in.

VI

We are plugged into a system that's sucking us dry, we're
selling our blood for peanuts, spinning it down for its
essence. You can shrug it off, of course, if you really
want to.

Hobo Bob is my Hope & Dream for us. To be the
friendly stranger that helps you change your tire late
at night in the rain,

or that special someone ahead of you in line at the
BuyMore who pays it forward, 'cause it's your turn,
pickin' up your tab with no thought of recompense.
Just for kicks. Ain't life grand?

VII

In the deepest sense Hobo Bob (or Hobo Bobette) is
us, ourselves, the folks on YouTube we see every day
who drop everything to free a puppy or an elk from
a muddy sink hole or save a struggling doe from
drowning in an icy lake.

Or who saves a child from a sealed-up car in the parking
lot sun.

Yeah, I better go ahead and break that glass. NOW.
Let the chips fall where they may.

These folks will thoughtlessly and immediately drop
everything to free a sea turtle found struggling, upside-
down on the beach, or a poor shore bird drowning in
a wasted drop of oil.

They will cut loose someone from a snare of plastic
fishing line or from another man's trash.

(That's our real legacy to the world, everywhere. We best
figure out right soon how to clean as you go.)
These Hobos amongst us leave no trace of their good
work, an unconscious karma yoga, and like good cops
they do their job then go.

They don't slather on their personalities, their mores or
their memes. They ain't sellin' anything and they don't
do it for the money.

There are plenty of skilled hobos and explorers out there
who just can't do their duly assigned tasks anymore.

VIII
But hold on. So sorry to ramble on like this, hearing
myself shout in my own ear, ranting as I write, even
if it is The Truth.

There's still enough time for us to run away, to catch
an empty coal car leaving the West Bottoms for cool
Californee real soon. Like right now.

Hurry up, dress warm, grab a bottle. We can be on the
beach in Venice, day after tomorrow.

We deserve it, boy howdy.

Hobo Bob Tells It Like It Is

*He's always talking about the light. He says it's a
Plotinian emanation of the unseen world.*
~ James Lee Burke

I

All the sages, actuaries, bookies, turf accountants,
campus tearaways, toffs, wide boys and our own court
astrologer, after long and delicate negotiations, have
finally come to an agreement.

They affirm that even one human manifestation on this
plane is so miraculous as to be virtually impossible.

In any event, regardless of our carefully calculated
odds and the current point spread, we present ourselves
here, in a reasonably timely manner, fresh from Mama's
warm succulent womb, screaming and bloody.

We spend the days of our lives trying to recreate an
adequate simulacrum of our time with her, to recapture
the calm beating of her heart, her warm salty fluid, and
sharing her deep dream-filled sleep of exhaustion.

All our future acts echo the lessons and habits acquired
in her narcotic, blood-warmed bath. As different as we
are, we all share this time,

and, indeed, it is the very ground of our being. It is in
this pool we truly learn to swim.

We are all deficient angels here, searching for that final
cool somewhere. The engine of cosmic chance has left
us so wanting, so needing.

Out of all this anxiety and confusion we are somehow driven to create around ourselves a flawed little empire of one.

Indeed, it is created by us, for us, with, of course, the inevitable leaden baggage of our energetic and karmic inheritance heaped up tall behind us.

We carry it on our little red wagon, or bound securely onto our sled, *Rosebud*. What a drag, Sisyphus, that long shadow we think we must always carry.

II
Indeed, we have invented our ten thousand gods to comfort and *illuse* us in the cold darkness of this vast multiverse. No intellectual rationalization can reasonably deny this.

So then why are we so afraid that we can neither return to, nor imaginatively reinvent Mother's amniotic sea? Try as we may.

Inevitably we fail in this, and we've evolved the neurotic personas that wander country lanes, back alleys, palace halls that have time and time again tried to justify every act of kindness, every crime, every kiss, every dream and every war.

Hence, all art, all civilization, all violence, all love and all madness. Other visible and invisible forces act upon us, of course, and there is certainly no respite from them this side of the grave.

III

We are as blind fish swimming in deep cave rivers, never
recognizing that it is in water we live. For humanity, the
vast universe is our water,

every drop from the deepest, silent, untouched and
most holy aquifer to the monstrous tsunami, crushing
cities onto new coastlines, all the way down to the
backed-up toilet in the reactor basement.

All is *Samsara*, the Buddhist web of illusion and delusion
that pulses and throbs around us here while we do our
little dance between naps. We are trapped by as well as
given life, energy and inspiration by it.

The fingerprints of our subconscious are on every act,
thought and fantasy, just as the subtle powers of the sun,
the planets, our moon and eternal gravity are.

Our beautiful and tragic tribe is eating up this world
as fast as it can, barely even trying to save it, ourselves
and the others speeding along with us.

These poems are but tiny doors into the world of me,
us and the shadow. There is only change. Language fails us,
and saves us.

Emptiness is fullness and noise. Just listen and see.
Read it and weep.

Hobo Bob's Valedictory

I
Thanks to everyone for attending this grand occasion,
especially my dear friends and confidants, way in the back
there, heading for the fire exit.

Also, I would certainly be remiss in not mentioning the
many representatives from the Office of Poetic Equity,
here with us tonight.

Their job is to assure that immoderate amounts of *poesis,
poesy,* and *poetiquette* are spread thickly across our big
wide world where it's needed now more than ever.

Frank Zappa, the late great genius, avant-garde composer,
guitar god, satirist and Presidential candidate, wrote in the
liner notes on one of his early albums. He declared,
no commercial potential, in latin, of course.

HaHa! We all laugh, so amused. But, alas, it's still
true. Frank said it so eloquently in the 1960's,
which, of course, we remember so well. Look
around you, a lot has changed. But Not That.

Poetry does not pay, except an occasional pittance,
plunked down into your tin cup, or worse, a fresh, clean,
ten-spot waved at you from the barely cracked window
of a shiny new Jag, holding up traffic that wants only to
speed by your cold and windy corner.

II

We're heading off, any second now, into our certain
specious demise, driven mad by the insane, malignant
heat-engine of late-stage capitalism. It's easy to see.
You just try living on nothing.

No shit & no surprise. We were all warned by certified
experts long ago. Me amongst 'em, proudly, a lifelong
victim of chronic and terminally comic *Schadenfreude*.

Unlimited growth and unblinking ideology is its *modus
operandi*. At the very top tip of its miles long to-do list:
Must Grow Bigger Faster!

This highly evolved parasite consumes its host and
itself until the inevitable unromantic and co-evolved
murder and suicide. Just like in the papers every day.

III

We gather here, today, as poets and artists, broke
down hard, hungry and thirsty for all that can and
should be granted to us as the *unelected legislators
of the world* that hard marks our truly unelectable class.

Of course, genius can be granted to us, any time really,
at a steep discount, of course, if only we 'fess up and
knuckle under to the giant machine at the heart of the
Matrix.

You touch its spinning wheels at your peril.
Watch your fingies!

IV
We stand here today and every day in the harsh light
of physical and biological law. Truly the *Tao*: entropy
and negentropy, all rolled into The Really Big One.

It operates seamlessly behind our proscenium's gossamer
veil, expressing the first and last rules of invisible global
eco-etiquette that constrain us all.

Everything runs down, (as far as we know) and *everything
is connected*. So keep up the good work, *Citizens*, fighting
inexorable entropy, just trying to get organized.

V
I'm so sorry but for us, it's much too late. We will all
be eaten, swimming across the burning Cuyahoga,
our Rubicon, as we head towards the horizon, hammer
and tongs in hand.

Perhaps, we in our nano-part, and the slick operators
behind the red velvet drape in their macro-part, have
transgressed The Laws of The *Tao* a trillion times too
often.

We all have known this. *Don't look so shocked.*
It seems a bit disingenuous at this late date.

As far as we know there is no way forward and no way
back, the classic double bind of hard science. The womb
shuts behind us, and here we are in the *Samsaric* rattrap
again.

Only the one door in—birth, parthenogenic or otherwise.
All doors out, locked, blocked and sealed up tight,
welded shut. *You only get a one-way ticket, pal.*

VI

Soon enough, money, memory, history and books will
vanish. Nothing will be left but the warm, gentle pitter-
patter of radioactive dust and toxic ash falling amidst
the wreckage of once great cities.

A few toppled bronzes may remain in the parks. Fallen
heroes, no doubt, and a nude muse or two. We can only
hope.

The First Folios, all Incunabula and the Old Masters
will be eaten by glowing roaches on once beautiful
Empire *fauteuils* in the dark shuttered palaces.

VII

And here we are, ending up, trapped in a system that
allows in way too much sunlight, more than enough
cosmic dust, gamma rays and the odd alien contraption.

Then, poor us, here only for a brief dance along the
Strand, just past the corner of Bush & Stockton,
Park Avenue, Rodeo Drive or The Paseo.

Or if rich, lucky and super fit, up a long cold corpse-
strewn stroll beyond Everest's Base Camp or on some
rough wooden plank ending abruptly above a shiny,
sunlit sea.

Either way we dance on into our glorious sunset,
just off Mulholland all aglow from the fires.

Hobo Bob Tells His Tale

I

There I was, born with a six-pack in each hand,
in a dirt-floored cabana out back, down by the river,
or so Mama said, Mama said.

Another legend has it that I was first seen ridin' an
old mule, a bright young Mama's boy comin' down from
Salisbury, Keytesville, Corder and Sparta,

passin' through on the road to The Big City, the psychic
dumpster of archetypes.

Upon my arrival, so I was told, I was taken in by wolves and
raised on corn pone, channel cats, bacon and taters, biscuits
smothered in rich sausage gravy, all dipped in maple *surple*.

I was fed fresh, daily ho-made snapping turtle fricassee
on the half-shell, road-killed and hand-plucked Yardbird,
awesome possum and b-b-cue'd horse pucky, down in the
basement of my alma mater.

II

My pets were all snakes in the grass, razorbacks, 20-to-a-
pack Wild Dogs, the last Great White Bison, Mr. Toad,
Froggy Gremlin and a coupla Jayhawks out on parole.

The lyrical modes of my tribe were big band blues, always
with full-sized horn sections. I can hear them now, beautiful
country bumpkins, Freddie Fender, Mel Tillis and ole Hank,
of course.

There was nary another white rocker in sight,
unless he was English, with a guitar and a dream,

and his cousin, another local boy made good, just
now seen bumpin' across the tracks, about Sunset,
drivin' crazy, with a mad look in his eyes,

headin' down Thunder Road, through Memphis, Nashville,
Cairo, plowed-up and salted Carthage, past old Sparta,
towards Del Rio to finally kiss that Big Game Ring.

III
Our jukebox only played all the collected speeches &
hard rockin' hits of my full-time corporate donors,
finally all pushin' up stones or in the prison choir singing
their little pea-pickin' hearts out to the Grand Jury.

IV
I leered and lusted after the All-American Girl next
door. And she me. A debutante of depravity she was,
and is, taut and shameless, a sweet young cheerleader
with a hankerin' for the Big Twelve and the NFL.

We could neither follow the rules nor stay on the bench,
Johnny. We much prefer the quiet life, back under the
bleachers, looking up at the stars.

Our children are all beautiful, perfect shots, drivin' the
little white ball right up onto the green in one.

V
So in spite of the above, in my long and blesséd life,
my demons, the poison garden spiders of *lust, greed,
depression, anxiety, insomnia* and *oral compulsion* have never
been fully exorcized.

Most likely they never will be now, given my fast
approaching sell-by date.

These six rugged demon-riders of mine,
a real wild bunch, came together last night,
out of the rain, burnished by lightening,
their horse's rain-soaked and shivering.

VI
I was drenched, in a cold, cold sweat, wrapped in a
long, black golden cape, nearly drowned in the spring
floods, already in deep, stranded on the roof of my
Town Car.

And now, lo and behold, just look what remains in
the wreckage of the retreating floodwaters but a newly
blossomed poem, washed up on the levee, freshly
hatched, red as roses and brightly bit lips, now near
full-grown and coming *atcha*.

Hobo Bob Dreams of Heaven

...entertaining angels unawares. ~Evelyn Waugh

Sure, heaven will be swell. All the great parties catered.
The napkins: Irish linen, huge and clean, for a change.

The Vatican's old silver is all laid out, spic and span,
squared away, just like in the Royal Navy.

There will be bunches of great bands, for sure.
No one up here cares what happens backstage
between sets.

The angels are fun at all these parties. They don't
talk back after a few cocktails like so many around here.

The dogs and cats have had their shots. They sleep
indoors if they want, and eat whatever, from the
endless buffet we all share.

Surely the weather will be swell up there. No storms
or rains or dangerous turbulent anomalies in sight.
Maybe a gentle Spring rain occasionally but usually
blue skies as far as Taylor's pilot can see.

No fucking mutual funds, either.

No need for cops, the army or government because
the locals there wouldn't put up with all that, the way
the suckers, rubes and marks do here.

It's hard to believe what is swallowed whole, holiday
wrapped and hogtied special every day in my
neighborhood.

Hobo Bob's Birthday Poems

So here it is rollin' by again, another birthday. And right
after the long celebratory lunch with my attorney, I'm
cruisin' back by the Wild Stallion Saloon for a cold glass
of red beer, celery stalk and a double shot to celebrate
spinning around our unimportant little star, keeping it
dizzily real, for one more year.

My initial entry, BirthDay One, was with a howl and a
yelp from those ice-cold forceps twisting my poor neck
something awful, to encourage my entry, Stage Left.

Similarly, years later, after a long happy life it all ended
for me, on a cushy hospital gurney as a large Samoan
cardiologist crushed my broken heart back into its
familiar rut.

Stunning, you say? Yeah, well, me too. But here I am, after
my salvation and resuscitation, still lusting after minor
muses and their pals, that have kept me, mostly, on the
straight and narrow all these years.

They've led me down the long broken yellow line to this,
my parking place in the sun. And such a glorious day it is,
too.

Those angels and goddesses, all my Muses, are up there
looking down from their classic porticos in the sky,
watching out for me.

Because it's my birthday.

Hobo Bob Sings About Long-Lost Texas

Seein' those bright lights of Dallas, feelin' that prairie
wind, watchin' those crazy wildflowers bloom. I'm in
Texasty again!

I'm seein' your smilin' face, lovin' your faded jeans.
Hold my hand now, baby, my head's beginnin' to spin.

I've sure missed the boys from Luckenbach and those
charmin' Houston debs. I drank deep of the Pedernales
and swam the Rio Grande, just beyond that fence.

I stopped by Cadillac Ranch to climb those twenty big
fins. But honey, without your wildfire lovin', how can I
ever win?

You can have your back East poodle shit and your
Hollywood *la-de-da*. All I want is my big Texan horsey,
and you, without end.

I've sure missed Lady Bird's bloomin' roadsides and
the whiff a cowpie brings. I miss those crazy cowboy
poets and the free-range rustler's grin. He's cookin' up
a whole beef side around the river's bend.

I can hear those lonesome longhorns callin' and the
near-by night birds cry. I'm in *Texasty*, livin' for that
prairie wind!

I dreamt of the smoke and shot at the Alamo and saw
our heroes fall. I dreamed of Bowie, and Davey, too.
I dreamt I saw it all.

And then, of course, I was at the Book Depository that
awful fateful day. Clear and fine it was in Dallas, where
nary a copper lied. I saw the second gun runnin'
and the bloodied wife who cried.

Hobo Bob Reports From Down by the Crick

Good news, boys and girls. Life and death abound here at the crick this morning. It's all part and parcel of that big package delivered fresh daily at every dawn's doorstep.

Gravity pulls this stream towards me from somewhere up near that time-rounded ridge upstream. It runs down through here over layers of flat rocks, stacked as if on purpose.

It meanders past me now, splashing over *the stones in my pathway*. Here and there are strong young frogs, a few still tadpole-ish, happy to be alive, hoppin' and cavortin', always underfoot. Unknowingly, they await their fate, and like me, seek refuge here beneath the shade trees.

The current of the rock-bottomed creek is strong, and flows quickly by. Its width, depth and wavelength are dependent on a very complex calculus of climate and weather, time itself and, of course, the planets above, spinning round and round.

The cold water eddies past my unsteady legs. Broken limbs and tree trunks have been forced up onto the banks during seasonal flooding.

The current pushed, pulled and scattered them every which way, but only as far as gravity will allow.

Continuing on downstream, I discover a rib bone and
a hard carapace bleached by the seasons, now all that
remain of small, former neighbors intertwined with me
in this web of life.

They're left behind, in confused profusion and I've
included them with my extensive notes, along with
untainted evidence gathered from the scene.

I describe it all here and report my findings to you,
otherwise engaged elsewhere.

Hobo Bob Dreamin' in the Rail Yard

I nod off, sitting here, gazing dreamily through my
train's flashing window. You gaze back from your
reflection and wave to us relaxin' in our recliners.

Across the void from us a long line of freight cars
rumbles past as we pull into the station, right on time.

The brakes squeal harshly all the way home. Nearly
there now—finally.

End of the line! Last call!, the conductor cries. His cars
all rack and roll and finally lurch to a stop with another
crying squeal.

The ghosts of Guys and Dolls Charlestoning in the
club car pass me, swingin' through my dream.

Hobo Bob Fishing the Same River Twice

I

It was Heraclitus, and not Hobo Bob, our guide, who said
that no one steps into the same river twice, and that every
river moves downstream forever,

and every Hobo changes every instant of every day that's
ever-changing around him, too.

Well, Sir, Hobo Bob wasn't around back then, I'm sure
of that. Right now he's somewhere nearby, usually found in
his leaky old waders knee-deep, or worse, in whatever body
of water's flowing by his unsettled feet.

Watch out! He's waving a long pole with a string and
a lure or a handmade fly hanging from one end. He's
trying to catch him, and maybe us, some fish.

Hobo Bob is *THE MAN* all right. He doesn't waste
much time reading entrails or reflecting on his lonely past
dragging him along the dusty path, like that shadow
behind him, always underfoot.

II

By the time our Sunset has disappeared into the shadows,
Hobo Bob will have caught us a mess of rainbow trout.
He'll have stashed them in his tattered wicker creel and
he'll have carried them fresh and cool, up the steep trail
to camp.

He'll have gutted, cleaned and grilled them up for us, before
our merry eyes. And we'll eat them, too, maybe with a side
of roasted taters, hot from the coals.

We'll happily clean our plates right there in the rushing
river laughing so prettily in the background.

The weary old philosopher and the distracted poet
won't miss this meal, that's for sure.
Appetite trumps cosmology every time.

III
But what a glorious day, huh? Up before dawn and
hard at it, we are. Hammer and tongs all damn day
long, framing up our tiny human experience.

Yup, I'm up, too, living large, then and suddenly tired
all those hours later. I'm off to bed after a coupla nice
grilled trout, cooked outdoors by someone else, over
hot coals under sparkling alien stars. Maybe there's even
a cool drink or two.

There's just not much time left after all that to make a
dent in these remorseless chores. Darkness comes at
ya hard. *What again*, you might ask.

It's the ultimate reminder of our mortality. Thank the
Gods it arrives sometime after a back-to-back high
tea and happy hour.

And, *gee*, it's swell to finally climb into my bed roll,
to pull the cool cover up over my head, then straight
down into dreamland, slip, slidin' away because any
second now:

surprise, surprise, good buddy, that old sun's gonna
pop up from somewhere East of Cape Ann,
behind those towering fluffy clouds.

IV

There will be a false dawn for sure, and it's time to start all over again. I can just now see in the first light that the heart of winter has broken, for the time being at least, for spring has many ways of fooling us.

The earth warms a bit in the morning sun and giant hungry lizards stir. They're now just South of the river and are beginning to make their way North, heading our way.

I see Hobo Bob down in the river again and I sure hope he's got a plan.

Bob on Bob

for Bob Dylan

> *You said you'd never compromise with the mystery tramp,*
> *but now you realize he's not selling any alibis.*
> ~ Bob Dylan, *Like A Rolling Stone*

Well, Bob, You've surely gone and done it this go-round.
You electrified those beatnik folkies. It was a real
shockeroo.

Yeah: Newport 1965.

You blew them clear into *the eternal now*, even way
back then. It was hard to handle. You could tell they
seemed upset.

You stepped up, like the Big Man, and pulled on
Woody's muddy old work boots. You filled 'em up
pretty damn good, I must admit.

And surely by now you've finally got a hold of Hank
William's old caddy ragtop. It's been up on blocks
behind some ruined roadhouse out along Highway 61,
passin' the time.

You're no Porter Wagoner or Bill Monroe, that's for sure.
But you've had plenty of hits, big ones at that.
Bigger even than Cole Porter.

The world has certainly gone on from there, I do
declare. It sure has. Check your *Twitter* feed or your X-File.
You'll see soon enough.

In any case, Bob, just keep pickin' and grimacin' the whole damn day,

and be sure to give Blind Willie McTell a big thumb's up when you bump into him down at the Crossroads.

Hobo Bob Lookin' for Spring

for ee cummings & Jonathan Swift, with fondness

It's been rumored amongst those in-the-know that
the powers-that-be will soon be bringing back lynching
from horseback, to discourage voters and to speed up
blind justice a bit.

Abortion and any family planning at all will soon
be finally exorcized nationwide by the Noble, Pious
and Holy amongst us, long determined to prevent
Love, Sweet Love from further spreading its anarchic
and riotous fright across our Sacred Land, now wholly
reclaimed from the Pagan Other.

Institutional disembowelment certainly will not be
far behind in a long line of powerful inducements
discouraging those that might, by chance or choice,
become a mite peckish and decide to snack or even
eat, late into the night while hungrily watching the
Great Leader do da do.

Then, finally, any and all windows that remain, will
be covered and sealed up tight as a drum, with thick
sheets of foreign steel, installed by certified, bonded,
desperate and groveling contractors to prevent folks
from defenestration,

trying only to get outside, to breathe in spring.

Hobo Bob's Morning at the Elk Ranch

I
It's morning again here at the Elk Ranch, uphill
from a dead witch tree hangin' over the crick.

Birds announce dawn's arrival early. They let each
other know their hopes and hungers for this brand
new day.

My big windows, open for the first time this year, are
lettin' in a gentle breeze. Our weather sure is swell,
here on the cusp of another perfect spring.

It's even better now that we've had a week of thunder-
storms passin' through, headin' East. I was beginning
to worry about how dry everything was.

It made me feel strange all over with the Age
Anthropocene ticking away outside my front door,
all the way down to the mailbox.

II
Most likely it will be the shortest age of them all, as there
will never be enough bean-counters around to change all
the batteries in our atomic clocks.

Yeah, and when those reactor pumps shut down and the
cooling ponds dry up, those giant cores will overheat,
catch fire and breach the holding tank walls.

Tainted boiling water will drain out into the river and run, glowing down to the sea. All the others too, will melt down in their own sweet time, without our people to look after them, and then, well, that's all she wrote. Forever.

But, hey, it's gonna' be a short day an' all, bein' a Sunday.

Hobo Bob Drivin' With Destiny

*We're both traveling bad roads and all bad roads lead
to bad towns.*~Ian Fleming, *Diamonds Are Forever*

I

Out West, where the roadkill smells rank along the right
of way, Destiny rides again. Out there water stands in
ditches—stinking and fetid. It's the fracker's dream.

Big rigs pick up speed heading West, faster and farther,
deep into yesterday's tomorrow. Our lonely national bison
gazes serenely at them passing, chewing on prairie grass
while standing guard at this off-ramp to the future.

The bones of the pilgrims, our forebears, picked clean
by the scavengers, are bleached by the ceaseless sun.
Cars and trucks lie about all cock-a-doodle,
abandoned by the roadside.

A hard-edged diesel dick, high-ballin' his 18-wheeler
overloaded with drillin' pipe, misses the tiny daisy
bloomin' in the median.

II

The top predator is behind the wheel, staring hard into
the rearview, white knucklin' it all the way home. He's
racing full-tilt for town, speeding towards that shimmering
mirage on the distant hills dead ahead.

We pass him, going the other way, pretty damn fast, too,
all the while twisting the cosmic dial way up to the
far end. We're takin' the long way 'round, waitin' for our
favorite song.

III

Over that spacey AM, Wolfman Jack is signaling to us
mysteriously from his post, deep inside Area 51. It's a
miracle we can catch any radio waves out here at all.

Through the static and space music we hear a bit of
ghostly Gene Vincent, Bob Wills, Howlin' Wolf, Lowell
Fulsom, Sonny Boy and John Lee. Boom, Boom.

There's our Holy Golden Book and a fully loaded
hog leg slidin' around on the dash in the afternoon
sun, both way too hot to touch.

There's a fresh plug of *Red Man* twixt teeth and gum.
There's a half-empty fifth of *Rebel Yell, rollin' and
tumblin'* under the front seat just outta reach.

IV

We're near empty, Man, and runnin' on fumes.
Mr. MoJo Risin' jumped out at the last Crossroad.
Better late than never, he said on his way out the door.

Out here every unlicensed handgun represents freedom
to someone. Every telephone pole a crucifix, every
lineman our savior.

Every hitchhiker is a cash cow inmate-in-waiting,
every bad tattoo a sportsman, every Marlboro Man
a politician and every politician a horse's ass,
out here cruisin' the super slab home.

Hobo Bob Homeless on the Range

The sleeping cowboy dreams of perfect hay bales,
his warm bunkhouse and a small medicinal whiskey
with spring water, taken on horseback, ridin' the dark,
lonely plain.

Clouds blow in over him shiverin' under his thin
saddle blanket. West to East they blow, crossing
the endless sky, at this hour filled only with stars.

His herd is there with him, hoofin' it. They wander
endlessly, munching their cud, having no thought
of the hammer, the trough and the sluice in their future.

Hobo Bob Lookin' for a Piece of
the True Cross

Jesus wept. ~ John 11:35

Jesus wept. Well, yes, I'll bet he did. We've all seen him
in the little golden books, looking up into his blue-eyed
heaven, watching, entranced in blessèd agony.

His hallucinations of pain play out across the red
Palestinian sunset one Friday afternoon before
a long weekend.

Perhaps he saw that sky filled with enchanting little
Baroque *putti* amongst those clouds, listening to the
pulchritudes of the angels whispering Daddy's message
into his shell-like ear: *Soon, soon, my will be done, Son.*

Who do you think he heard, hangin' around up there
on his cross made from the Genesis Garden tree?
What songs? What cantos of lyric epics? I'll bet it was
Pan playing those lyres and golden pipes.

Perhaps Sirens sang to him as they sang for Odysseus,
tied to his ship's mast by his crew, their ears, wax-
plugged against the hypnotic song.

Of course, Odysseus had to know, had to hear, had to
see and, yet, still not be swept away. He was who he
was and more adventures waited just over the horizon.

But did those guys ever tell what really happened?
Did they pass their messages on to anyone?

It's doesn't seem likely. Some things just don't add up.
I've found nothing in Homer or the Holy Book to suggest
anything specific. It was a secret for them alone.

It was their trip. Not ours.

Hobo Bob Drops by the Dog-N-Suds

Your name came up in a conversation I overheard
this afternoon at the *Dog-N-Suds*.

I was sitting there in the sun minding my own business,
quietly making a mess of my super huge double-dip
drippy cone.

I heard the couple at the next table mention your name
in hushed tones. Not that that is so unusual.

They said that you weren't sure what you were going
to do and that the fella in question wasn't sure either.

It doesn't seem all that different from the usual but
I thought you should know.

Please keep us in the loop as to your decision, if things
change. We are concerned.

What's-his-name will have to work it out on his own,
I guess.

Hobo Bob Choking As He Chews

Three squares just don't cut it for this guy.
He eats all the time.

He confronts every neurotic proclivity
with an open mouth.

Careful! He'll eat you out of house and home.
(No wonder my fridge is always empty.)

If I buy it, he eats it. Right on the spot.
In the car.

Standing at my sink. Right after lunch.

Hobo Bob the Kitchen Cuckold

for Anthony Bourdain, 1956–2018, RIP

> *Dull food, but immaculately cooked.*
> ~Dame Miriam Rothschild

Now I am truly heartbroken. Everything was going
along just fine, and then outta the blue we heard about
Tony's tragic suicide.

So, my girlfriend, after this tough news, so hard to
swallow, casually cuts me deep, from across the living
room, and so nonchalantly too.

He really did it for me, since the first day I laid eyes on him.

Her words went in from the back, smooth as an ice pick,
low down, up between those fatty ribs,

deep into those fresh, still somewhat tender sweetbreads,
as I stood over the sink, doin' my job.

Yes, indeedy. She admitted that she had been in love
with him, forever and a day. I never knew.
How could I have known?

She'd loved him in secret for years, long before he was
a star, the world-class vagabond epicure that he became,
pointing out his way to us, so eloquently.

That obviously doesn't leave much room for me, does it,
here between the coffee pot and the colander?

So, whoa, I guess now I'm the kitchen cuckold and the bus boy, playin' the fool again.

Where did they meet? *Waffle House?* It's the only possible place in this horse-less backwater town. There's nowhere around here to even get decent bar food.

And yet, here I am, standing by the soapy dish-filled sink, *Le Jerque*, a deeply wounded pearl diver.

How long has this been going on?, I hum, covering the pain of realization, my apron damp with tears.

True love will out, I guess. *And romance is mush.*

How could I tell her that I had loved him, too, in my own way, of course, especially since Chet Baker left the building so suddenly.

But here I am, happy to clear the table, to empty the dishwasher, now that I know how,

and, like Eddie Haskell, or Lumpy, I get the trash out just in time, regardless of the weather.

Hobo Bob Seals the Deal

I

I saw you down at the Crossroads the other night.
No, not the one with the toné galleries stretched
out for miles along the Boulevard. The other one.

You know full well the one I'm talkin' about.
It's that place where the soft buttery moon is always full,
hangin' above the misty swamp. It's the color of a wolf's
eye, round, and winkin' back at us, laughin' all the way.

Odd numbers of ravens circle above, counter-clockwise,
countin' down our remaining time tick, tick, tickin' away.

II

And, there you are, kneelin' down in your grubby
black-striped jammies, shackles cast aside, escaped at
last from Parchment Farm. Giant hounds howl in the
distance, headin' this way.

It musta been somewhere *'round midnight*, crickets
fightin' bullfrogs to share center stage with that
yellow-eyed moon.

Your stingy brim's pushed way back, your sweat reflects
the light shining off your brow. You're talkin', not
declaiming as usual, but more like a brave negotiation.

I can't hear your words from down here in the coulee.
But I sure can see what's goin' on.

There's nobody there for you to talk with, and you do
carry on. But you're kneelin' in the muddy Crossroads
on Highway 61, starlight comin' through the trees.

Your voice rises and falls. Furtive clouds blow across
that old devil moon. I didn't follow you. No way. I'm playin'
the hand I dealt myself long ago.

You're rantin' now, speakin' in tongues, then,
suddenly you're quiet, your head down.

Then I see you get up, grab your tow sack and
head down the road. With purpose, I do declare.

III

When you've finally gone 'round the bend, I catch my
breath, sneak on up, as my heart, it jumped into my mouth.
A woman, all in whispering white, steps to the center
of the road from outta' the swamp.

The crickets stilled. The frogs stop croaking. Heat
lightning flashes behind the clouds. A freight train
cries out its song in the distance. Even the braying
hounds fall silent.

She softly whispers my name in a voice like a song
handwritten with my tears. Dumbstruck, I fall into a
dark puddle there.

The last thing I see, before I pass out, is two pair of
boot prints: yours, heading West, the other pair heading
back into the dark swamp.

IV

Then, I awoke with a start, refreshed and hungry,
in the French Quarter's octoroon dawn,
my fondest wish in hand, and a deep crossroads cut
in my right thumb.

Blood everywhere. I guess it's from where I pressed my
thumb down real hard on the big vellum page, to seal
the Deal.

Hobo Bob Tells Us Not to Wait

Gone fishin', instead of just a wishin'.~Harold Ensley

Just tell 'em I've gone fishin' way out beyond the reef.
Tell 'em I'm takin' a long rest from this fleshy mess.
Tell 'em I won't be back anytime soon.

But perhaps one day after a trip to Davy Jones' Locker,
I'll return, swept in on the pounding surf
as driftwood. Or a coconut.

Maybe I'll end up sprouting there in the sun, growing
out of the rocks, watching sailboats sunning in the harbor,

listening to the eternal waves crash on my beach,
and to the Sirens whispering through my leaves.

Johnny Reb Visits Hobo Bob and Gets a Lecture

All your buried corpses begin to speak. ~ James Baldwin

I
I don't know what to do. Fireworks are going off
in all directions.

BANG! BANG!—BANG!

Out the front door down the hill towards town.

BANG! BANG!—BANG!

Up the hill to the West, past the ancient barn,
the giant elk, the lonely horse, towards the
vanishing sunset.

BANG!—BANG!—BANG!

After an early rain, gray fog and blue smoke from
the celebration next door rolls towards me along
the old road that's been in use here now for two
hundred years.

II
It's carried plenty of dirty feet in muddy boots,
long dresses and satin slippers; cars and trucks,
carts, carriages, tractors and trailers; horses, cows, elk
and dogs, giant bales of hemp and, alas, slaves.

The smoke, it's thick. I can barely make out
Johnny Reb slouching his way outta the

darkness, comin' towards me, standin' in the
lantern light by the door.

The explosives entertaining the living today have
somehow awakened the dead of yesteryear and
have brought them back to us through the gray
smoke.

III
I just don't know what to tell him when he stops by,
to ask for a drink of well water and a namesake
Johnny Cake.

Sure, I will dip up some water for him and wrap
some fresh cake in a flour sack from the mill in
town, for his long trip onward, to where no one
knows.

IV
But I'm not sure if we will even speak the same
language anymore. What can I tell him of the latest
news hereabouts?

That his side lost, that they keep losing, that they will
always lose? That he and his people were duped,
then and now, have been duped all along. That black
people are free, barely, and that Oxycontin is the
new King.

That the damned victorious Yankee flag has been
dragged through so much offal, blood, bones, and has
wasted so much stolen beauty, youth, our gold and
their lives, in its name, so much more than can ever be
counted.

Our noble dead have been piled up 'round the world like
cordwood in an Ozark fall. Those Yankee carpetbaggers
will do business with anyone, preferably the most depraved
amongst us because they are so easy to recognize,
like looking into our golden mirror.

V
We are so proud of our dead on this day of our
hideous self-love, so proud of our dark racist dreams,
proud of women, and *indigeneros* in their place and
little girls ripe for the pickin'.

I guess the only good news for Johnny is that he can get
his five-and-dime flag any-proud-where. He will not
even recognize it.

Oh, yeah, and, uhh, Johnny, we still love blowing shit
up, here in North Dixie.

Hobo Bob Contemplates His Own Mortality

The nights, the days, the dark, the light. Ho hum.
It's life and life only, as Bobby D. sang so lyrically,
once upon a long, long time.

The dream unfolds, the bubbles burst. The slender
moments rattle and gong like bamboo stalks on
ancient Chinese scrolls.

At dawn a skeptical old bullfrog glares up at me
from just beneath the empty mirror of a pond
we share. He shows no fear.

But then again, no one is afraid of white men,
when first they meet. But just you wait, Froggy Gremlin.

We come as friends, bearing many gifts, stuff you
don't have and might not have after we leave.

All in all, the only ones who will finally win are the
deathwatch beetles and, of course, *the conqueror worm.*

Hobo Bob Gets a Glimpse of the Gold

We seem born to the quest, don't we? There's no rest
from it either, except perhaps briefly.

It seems to be worked out nightly in our dreams,
where we search for clues, like panning for gold
in the backwaters of life's rushing stream.

Golden flakes settle as the water flows by us sitting on
the bank, entranced, boots wet way above the ankle.

The sound life's stream makes is music. It whispers,
chats, sings and declaims: a half-remembered love song,
a poem, some beautiful fragment or other.

It's impossible to know what all it says or means.
Translation is a delicate art, and a science. It's not
easy to learn the subtle language of water on rock.

You look hard through everything for a glimpse of
those twinkling golden clues. Perhaps there will be
something to take home from the long day after all.

Hobo Bob Contemplates the Vernal Equinox

I
It's nice hearing a bit of rain on the roof during the night.
I awoke in time to see our only moon rise, again.

The astronomy wags call it the first New Moon after the
Vernal Equinox. It's the same old new moon to me.

But now that it's finally dawn and it's so sweet seeing
everything green again, and fecund like it used to be.

From every seasonal crick running with rain, life springs
forth.

We had a great lightnin' storm too, jiggin' and jaggin' across
the cloud-covered valley, West to East into the new day's
dawn.

I caught it all relaxin' on the front porch. It could easily
have been Camarillo.

II
This latest storm blew in from the opposite direction
of the pilgrims and pioneers. They rolled through
once upon a time, Conestogas loaded for bear, they only
needed to pick one famous trail or another, then head out.

It wouldn't be long before they were cutting across someone
else's big backyard.

Our antecedents expected this rite-of-passage as their
god-given due, of course, along with a nice basket lunch

prepared in town, cold chicken wrapped in gingham
plaid, a fashionable beaver hat,

and a swell parcel of priceless first growth timberland or
un-ever fenced tall-grass prairie with water rights intact.

By god, they got it too. All of it. But ever since then,
dragging along behind them in the shadows are a
hundred million ghosts wandering perpetually through
their dreams.

Yeah, you can never tell what's coming down the pike,
especially these days: the next war, the latest shark bite,
or *a brand new baby day* now grown up and moved away.

Right on time, too, because here comes another one,
just like the other one.

Hobo Bob Rejects It All, Finally

Having to live up to the fantasies of others is a real drag.
~ Chet Baker

I
I want to let you know that, as of this morning,
right now, this very instant, I'm demanding of all
and sundry a full reinstatement of my inalienable
birthright to loaf, goof off, or for that matter,

to lounge about expressing my slackness, or to
kick back, to throw or flip my flops. It's the same
with shoes or boots.

II
This morning, so far, I'm barely out of bed and
in this brand new day, I've resolved to cast off
the need to be accountable to any man, woman,
beast or billy goat,

in any way, shape, manner or form, in whatever style
or substance, wherever they might hail from,
for whatever reason or season.

III
Furthermore, I'm demanding a full and complete
release from all the to-do, the to-be-done, the why-
and-the how, and all the-how-de-do.

If any of this pulls your chain too hard, go ahead
and stop that check. Or put a check in the mail
if you are so inclined to express your support.
Why wait?

Either way, I could not care less. I've no more truck
with all the hurry-up-and-go. Already I'm way late
according to somebody else's schedule. *So what?*

And as of this very instant: I don't do pressure, not even
a little bit. Shit's gonna get done somehow or other.
It will all happen in its own sweet time, or meantime
or kindtime. And as of today not on my time.

I won't even bother to figure out what will happen
to the world when it gets my memo demanding
full and complete release from any and all sufferance.

And as of right now, no more chores, darlin'. I just
called Big Daddy on the Spirit Phone to let him know
that *School's Out Forever.*

IV
Since I've already cast off my shoes and socks, I'm
gonna' cut across the big sky pasture barefoot, right
in front of those heifers and steers, to make my way
through the ass-tall, Johnson Sawgrass, to the big barn.

You just go on ahead and try to find another sucker or
loser who hasn't figured it out yet and who hasn't
bothered to look at him or herself up close, in whatever
mirror is in their handbag, man-purse, or covered up by
that old feed sack hangin' behind the barn door.

But, never mind all that right now. Instead let's roll
that old Lincoln outta the barn, wipe the dust off that
vintage tuck & roll, pull that ratty ragtop down and get
some highway wind in our great hair on the long road
to *that final cool somewhere.*

Since we're already headin' that way, let's pull over at our favorite old roadhouse and have us a coupla rounds apiece since it's always Happy Hour there.

V

Let's spend some quality alone time there, in our favorite corner booth, tryin' to recalculate our *quantum necessariorum* on a coupla handy bar napkins.

Show your work. If you feel up to it, that is.

Hobo Bob Isn't Worried About
the Paragons

*paragon: a model of excellence; sometimes referring to exemplary
members of a species, often the long-lived, survivors*

It will be a day like this, maybe a tad warmer, not a
cloud in the sky, when our heroes finally chopper
outta here off the Embassy roof.

Theirs is a big job, a mission on behalf of planetary life,
certainly without hope.

The standing orders will be to cool down the overheated
reactor cores, soon to be blowing off steam and
irradiated hot water.

The big ones, the remaining paragons, livin' in rivers
downstream from the reactors, those that remain,
were here long before us.

They hide upstream from dams and bridge abutments
in darkness, mud, weeds and lithic scatter.

Facing upstream, mouths wide, eyes closed, somnolent,
barely moving. They aren't listening and don't care.

They wait patiently for lunch to come their way, which
it will. It always has, for millions of years. Count on it.

We have the clocks. They have the time.
Any ingested isotopes will only make them stronger.

Hobo Bob Eatin' American Party Food

You know what they say about this place?
All you can eat for $300 bucks.
~Ian Fleming, *Diamonds Are Forever*

I

Hey, Hey, Escoffier, tonight we're talkin' about American
Party Food! So belly up to the huge buffet, and look out,
here comes that desert cart rollin' our way, right now,
across this grand old dining room.

But you know, really: nothing satisfies like beef, to go with
a nice big slice of pie. It's a *huuge* pie, too, but only a few
ghetto elbow their way up to the trough.

But oh, that beef: so richly marbled, and all wheel drive
loaded up fresh each dawn onto monster trucks at the
rural feed lot camps. It's delivered cold and rare, to the
urban camps, always open and waiting breathlessly.

Yeah, we're all eatin' American Party Food. It's a lifestyle
thing. *It's just business.* Hey, the middleman and the
little guy gots to eat and make a buck, that cute bus boy
bending over the back bar, the goddess, your server.

The salesman sellin' you additives. The crop duster
sprayin' your bugs and your kids, flyin' off into the setting
sun. They all gots to have a job 'cause all those farmers
can't live without us.

Everyone must eat. Eat to live or live to eat? Your plate
and bowl, cup and saucer: half empty or half full or over-
flowing the lip into your lap and all over that nice tie.

There are always seconds and thirds to go 'round.
Take some home. Open 24/7. Come on down.

II
Be sure to get a clean plate when you return to our
buffet 'cause it's The Law. There's always a second
chance to scarf it up here at Buffet America, that is,
if ya got da ticket.

Boy, it sure tastes good now, right now. It's everywhere,
that Party Food, clean new plastic utensils at the big
picnic of life.

III
I really only need one tool and that's my mouth.

How long can I go without food? Actually, to tell the
truth? Not all that long. However, right now I'm cuttin'
it back to about eight or ten thousand calories per diem,
starting tomorrow. That's all I need to barely get by.

I start off my day with acoupla big boxes of hot
office donuts, backed up with at least a dozen cups of
industrial strength coffee, *till death do us part,*
to get my morning off the ground. I mean *woke!*

I usta drink with both hands, as fast as I could, mouth
wide, sucker and straw. But there's not much chance
to quit eatin' American Party Food. It's so affordable.

I can't quit. My one vice. What, you say? Yeah, well,
maybe right after lunch.

Food is the greatest business. It's a hellofa markup,
the greatest return on investment. Better than bullets.

And fuck the help. They're people persons. There will
always be another starving sucker standing in line,
with their mimeographed application in hand, ready
and able to become a Member of the Team.

They stare through the paw prints on the big window,
right outside at the always-open-never-closed, *Buffet
America.*

IV
Go ahead, pack those dumpsters with your leftovers, that
stinkin' kitchen trash, the weekend grease trap harvest.
Dump all your dawn ashtrays and dirty sheets right here,
right now.

We'll haul it off to the evergreen fairway landfill. We
can't have that mess layin' about everywhere.

Folks don't wanna see what was on their plate once
upon a time, just a holiday office party minute ago.

*Not in my backyard. Get it outta here. It's almost
Christmas. Empty those shelves. We need the room.*

Regardless, it's gonna move on up the food chain, chain,
chain. Let's go ahead and turn the world into *another dirty
toilet in hell.*

It's easy. *It's just business.* It's all spelled out right here
in our big, thick and approved business plan, and the shiny
new Constitution.

Build it up, flip it for the quick buck, hit the silk,
bail on *the suckers and losers,* leave them holding

a big bag of chicken necks and shitty leftovers,
while we're already headin' South.

V
Of course, I'm totally down with all that, for sure,
but I'm gonna be really busy until right after lunch.

But go ahead and call in my order will you please?
I want a coupla big bypass burgers, with everything,
of course, including the kitchen sink. No tip on my
check. It just encourages them.

And, dear God, I've had such a mighty hankering for
those red-hot chimichangas all morning, and pickled
okra and a big bowl of super hot chili with beans,
day-old fresh, right off the big grill on the patio,

and calf fries, and pickled herring in dill sauce, just like
Daddy, up late one night, all ready to go-go-go *in the
cold gray dawn.*

And don't forget a pound or two of Granny's ho-made
nut fudge and be sure to see your hostess-with-the-
mostest, on your way out the door.

She'll get your carry-out order all packed up and ready
to go, then we can blow this pop stand. I'll be revin' up
our big muscle car right out front.

Hobo Bob Shares the News

I

As the world speeds up and we wind down, it's all trick or
treat and happy landings. Its end is like its beginning,
just the *B* side echoing those same old power chords.

But it's not over quite yet. And at this exact moment,
it looks like the bad guys won. Too bad, so sad.

Their party's just begun, all that loot and plunder stacked
sky high, up and down Fifth Avenue, and in Pondicherry,
their yachts have just been released from impound,
cleared customs, now all fueled, warmed and waiting
at Pier 13.

II

I doubt, however, that they will get very far in the end.
Their wars are all nearly over, the newshounds tell us so.

Tomorrow is the weekend, and it's Christmas to boot.
Another lump of coal on the kitchen fire and the house
of cards will combust.

Not your fault. Out of your control.

The glaciers all melt on our long misread maps,
and both Venices sink in Saturday's sun.

Hobo Bob Runs Into Mr. Mojo Risin'

for Jim Morrison & friends interred in le Cimetière du Père-Lachaise, Paris

Jimbo, *Mr. Mojo Risin'*, is out there now, making his
rounds, wandering the hills and dales, creepin' the
tourists just for grins, checkin' his flowers. He pays
cordial visits to his long-time neighbors.

He hangs with them: versifyin' with Stephen Spender,
yakking it up with Mezz Mezzrow about the good times
in Old New Orleans, relivin' the Second Line.

He sings duets with Maria Callas, teaching her the
blues, as if he could teach her anything about the blues.
She's so patient with him.

He's got time on his hands now, and knows everyone
on his block. It's so restful here. He's mellow now, he
fits right in.

His performance anxiety has all drained away like tiny
raindrops hitting grave marble on a Parisian afternoon.

Apollinaire, Oscar Wilde and he sit around their
favorite haunted mausoleum, groovin' on the total *dAdA*
makeover of the universe, in the rising lights of another
blood-red moon.

There is more than one belly laugh at this meeting.
There will be an eternity of them.

Hobo Bob Considers His Legacy

When my time finally flickers and fades, they'll bust
down the door to harvest all the snapshots, pictures
of the kids and a few tiny poems outta this tired old
brainpan, exhausted and energized by so many years
of, well, *livin' the dream.*

The friendly technicians will upload my stories, sad
and glad, as well as all the little unscripted cinematic
clips of days gone *bye-bye,* that rest here, scattered
all over the floor, a real mess.

But for the moment, I'm still breathing in the black
smoke of internal combustion and exhaling the
fragrance of daffodils into every *brand new baby day.*

It's a long and complicated story-line, now only
beginning to make sense.

It's High Noon and Hobo Bob Hits
the Road, Hard

Leaving the big box shop, desperate for more,
I head out into the slowly spinning rotisserie world.

Their revolving doors keep spinning, for sin and sinner alike.
They still don't have what I want.

Not one damn thing amidst the ten thousand things.

I'm burdened by these thoughts, (and bagless) as
I hurry out to my cabriolet, locked up tight,
upholstery smokin' in the shadeless sun.

Shaking my head, I think: *We've really done it this time.*

I crank'er up, pull away fast, puttin' my lead foot
into it, jumpin' the curb, smokin' my new tires,
as I speed into the traffic jam idlin' dead ahead.

I'm bakin' in the broiler, fryin' pan in the fire.
AM radio up loud, playin' somethin' hot, I wait.

Hobo Bob's Thirst Unquenched

Once upon a morning in my Minnesota youth, I caught
a tiny skink, a *Plestiodon fasciatus*, I believe.

I imprisoned him in an old tobacco tin, courtesy of
Prince Albert. That skink became a prisoner of love,
because he was mine: finders, keepers, losers, weepers.

Or so I thought. He didn't even make it to lunch, dying
of a tragic, thirsty loneliness that I seem to have contracted
from him during our short time together.

It was, perhaps, a curse upon me on his last summer's day.
Somehow ever since I've managed to stay out of hot tin
boxes left in the sun.

But my bottomless thirst remains unquenched to this
very day

Hobo Bob Advises Us

I'd say I've moved into a whole new era, for sure. It's a
full-blown blinker this time. My old buddy referred to it
as a phase shift.

He said it's like that time we'd been drinking cold beer
all afternoon on Victor's front porch, in the hot sun,
and then at about Happy Hour, we started on shots
of *mescal con gusano*.

He said: *Now, that's what I call a phase shift.*

This most recent phase just passed. It's rambled on a
while, at a leisurely pace with a moment for a fellow to
catch his breath,

a peaceful moment or two in the garden to gather his
rosebuds, to give himself and them a clean break:
The Pause That Refreshes.

But lately, the phases have ratcheted way up: fast, much
faster. You may know what I mean.

Indeed, it's already another long weekend and a whole
'nother notch up, so we're now long beyond the blink,
blink, blinking phase.

But now I've passed into another, strange interval. Clicking it is. Click. Click. click-click, click-click, and now, mid-day, mid-week, mid-year, there is no end in sight.

Click-click, click-clock.

Hobo Bob Was Tempted

I'm not thinking much about you these days,
not even-a-little. Or ever, actually.

Well, hardly ever. But no, not never-never.
Or not never-whatsoever, either.
And, no, not-no, no-no, not no-never-no.

(But on that dreamy afternoon in June, we spooned.
Not-ever gonna think-think about what we did-did.)

No way. Not this-way or that-way or any which-way.
Or if you were tempted, too. Also. But no, never-not
never-ever.

No, really, and not ever-never.
No way, José. No how, brown cow.

Certainly not this way. Or that-way, not-today.
Not this-day, or any other not this-day,
and most certainly not that-way-day.

Neither any-day, either. Ever. Or that some-day-
after-tomorrow, what-so-ever.
And don't bother to write. Or call. Or message.

Or text. Or pretty-FaceTime. Or rant-on-line.
And, of course, please, Sweet Jesus, don't visit.
I might never let you leave. Never-ever.

Hobo Bob Ridin' the Rails

It's tricky hopping a freight at dawn down in the rail yard,
but once you do—look out!

They do pick up speed, those trains.
Click-a-dee-clack, click-a-dee-clack, click-a-dee-clack.

Suddenly there you are, out of the yard, and into the
world, picking up speed, rolling and lurching side to
side, along the rocky railbed. Hold on!

By then it's way too late to jump, no matter what.
Your destination and your engineers are the same.
On this trip, anyway. He just doesn't know it yet.

Already he's dreamin' of his thermos of black coffee,
his lunch bucket and the warm roundhouse waitin' at
the end of the line.

Click-a-dee-clack, click-a-dee-clack, click-a-dee-clack.

Outta the yard and into the world. Across the bridge,
over the river, outta the big city and into the big sky
country that opens up to let the stars in.

Click-a-dee-clack, click-a-dee-clack, click-a-dee-clack.

You pass those no-name depots, those small empty
towns all the same, nights black as coal, or fuel oil.

No lights in dry *arroyos* under desolate old bridges
along your way.

Click-a-dee-clack, click-a-dee-clack, click-a-dee-clack.

Your car rolls past unlit. At lonesome crossroads,
redneck trucks wait, unsafe at any speed, and
those midnight riders, dream of their great escape.

Click-a-dee-clack, click-a-dee-clack, click-a-dee-clack.

Hobo Bob Reporting From the Back Roads

Cruising around here is mostly confined to the lonely
highways and back roads leading me in circles.

Little animals, and the not-so-little, crisscross these
country roads, fields and forests, finding their way,
through instinct and sharp eyes, day and night.

They know where they're going. They were here
first and don't even know we exist.

At last count I've saved seven jaywalking turtles
so far this year. Some big boys: a snapper or two.

Passing trucks barely slow. Some honk, brazenly.
Not one fuck given, and no thanks, either.

A big doe, surely someone's Mother, lies by the road-
side in a ditch, as I blow by.

Then, of course, *down the road apiece*, I saw her big
buck, somebody's Daddy, of course, dead as a doornail.

His broad back was jammed up into the barbed-wire
fence separating his land from theirs.

Hobo Bob Catches a Nasty Split-Finger

When I'm home, I eat right off the plate, standing
over the sink, mouth full, choking as I chew.

And now I am workin' someone else's clean-up
roster. I knew I should be getting that cold beer
for some guy callin' the plays from deep in the
rec room downstairs.

And some peanuts, you knucklehead!

But here I am hangin' around the sink, big as the
infield, filled with hot, soapy water, casually dreamin'
of a coupla chili dogs all my own.

As I was mindlessly washing up, suddenly, from out in left
field, I felt the wet pitcher slip. I reached for it and missed
by a mile. It dropped slick, wet and fast, smashing right
onto the big plate right there.

I saw it drop down—fast and low. The pitcher and
the plate bounced right past my empty cup.

There wasn't a thing I could do.

Here I was, the kitchen catcher, standing over the plates
and saucers, all wet, unmasked, nowhere near the action.
It seemed so easy, too.

For sure, it was quite an error: to be unseen forever by the
ump, the madding crowd, the gang in the rec-room even
in replay.

Besides everybody is way too busy watching a real game on the Jumbotron. I can hear them roar. It was another great play, I guess.

I'd timed it perfectly, reaching way out to catch that pitcher, to save it, the plate and the game.

They hurtled untouched through time and space towards their ultimate collision.

I saw them break sharply, right in front of me. I'd muffed it, big time. I kept replayin' it over and over in my head.

All I caught was a nasty split-finger on my ungloved, throwin' hand. I moved back sharply, stepping on broken crockery and glass.

I threw off my glove and ran to the infirmary to bandage up my cut, quick. The show must go on.

In spite of all this pain and excitement, I hurried back to clean up the mess, to get that guy's beer and nuts before the owner comes down from her Skybox.

Hobo Bob Was Right After All

He told me, in a quiet moment, once upon a time:

I
As I look back on my life, I realize that, more or less,
I have been right about the things that matter and
wrong about the rest.

I now understand that all beings are first-class
passengers, that any and all implied rights, accrue to
everyone. And most of all, no one is free until all of us
are free.

II
Yet somehow we still think we're immune from the
invisible forces pushing us around. The inevitable push
and pull of the endless tides and our earth's orbit
influence us mightily,

yet we continue to live our lives as if they will never
end and that wallpaper will cover the cracks.

III
I was right about the invisible, that nothing is as it
seems, and that all life depends on little beings we
walk over and breathe in every day that don't even
know we exist,

and that every man, woman, child and puppy dog
travels through here, so often as unrealized avatars
embodied to accomplish incredible feats of legerdemain.

IV

I was right about loving you, even as I saw your her,
trapped in those fabulous eyes still young,
still mischievous, half a century on down the line

My remaining dream is to grab hold of you,
or whoever I thought you were, or might become,
and to never let go, in spite of everything.

He Left Me a Note

One afternoon, on a clear day, Hobo Bob and I were
out on the Lake, *tipplin' a jar*, wettin' our whistles
and our fishin' lines simultaneously, when out of the
blue, he said,

You know, he left me a note. It said:

> *My gun is my friend. This hog-leg never saw a bullet*
> *it didn't like. It's there for you, on the sideboard in*
> *the library. Shoot your shot. Pull your trigger.*
> *Clean your weapon.*

He had had it layin' about for years and used it to plink
away, to scare the occasional crow or raven caught
red-handed in his pea patch.

He had been a lawman early-on, but was certified mad
at a young age. Anywho, they let him keep his badge.
He found it comforting, I guess, and the Sheriff didn't mind.

He came and went through the years, and my life,
like the tides and the seasons. I always wondered
what made him tick.

The last time I saw him was one summer evening
a while back, in an idling black and white out in the drive.

He sat quietly, leaning forward, his hands folded behind
his back, like they do when cuffed. Of course, the
deputies had known him for years.

I stepped up towards the open window to say something:
maybe goodbye, when the kindly deputy stopped me
a couple of feet from the cruiser and quietly said,

Son, best say your goodbyes from here. He's calm now,
but any little thing might set him off. He's touchy this
evening.

Who could blame him, I thought. The officers finished
their business and were soon gone.

I went up on the porch to watch the black & white
roll down the hill, and at the end of the long drive,
turn slowly onto the highway.

Their flashing red light was on and spinning,
but there was no siren to disturb the peace.

Hobo Bob Always Threatened

I

Hobo Bob sometimes threatened to rustle up a string
of ponies to herd down your way, overland,
navigating the dry *arroyos* by starlight.

We never really took Bob seriously. He didn't seem to have
it in him, when push finally came to shove. Under what
sky would he need a string of ponies? It's beyond me,
especially since he's left a vintage Indian motorcycle in
our barn.

He had traded his old Lincoln ragtop to some folkie who
cruised through here a coupla years back, tired of the
biker's life on the road, bugs on the teeth, now wanting
to travel in style for a change. You know, *movin,' groovin,'
doin' it.* Something classy, with suicide doors, to keep his
guitars in.

II

Bob says he still wants to get down your way soon,
to relive the glory of the Old West, wild or otherwise.
The reality of it was much rougher, I expect.

More likely: too hot, too cold and deadly boring most
of the time. Crosswise winds whistling through chinks
in what passed for dwellings back then, drivin' folks mad,

or sometimes hearing random gunfire out in the street,
or *home on the range,* shot through the thin veil of peace,
every time.

III

I finally gave Bob directions to your place. *My bad.*
So don't be surprised if late one night, you awake with
a start, hearing what might be that old Indian in the
distance, grindin' its way up the rugged trail to your
place.

Bob always loved the idea of the West. But you know
how easy it is to overlook the bad shoes, worse boots
and broken Conestogas abandoned along the trail.

IV

Hobo Bob never lets history get in the way of truth,
like so many of us. Everyone seems to forget it's pretty
much been a classic Western all along. Somehow, by
pure chance, we've found ourselves with this tiny bit part.

With no script in hand you wander onto the set from
out of the sun, leading a tired and thirsty horse
right into the heart of the action, for just a second,

and to perhaps leave your body amongst the dead or
wounded in the daily cinematic gun battle, high noon
at Boot Hill.

V

I told Bob that it would be easier on him, and us, to
keep it simple: order us all another round, then pick up
his old hat and coat, his brindle'd staff, then
head out through those big swingin' doors, down into
the empty street to turn left at the Crossroads, and head
due West, come what may.

Hobo Bob on His Way out the Door

I

After my turn in the barrel, when I'm finally put out
to some institutional pasture, I might one night out
of sheer boredom or desperation cry out for a priest.

Or priestess, even better.

In those dark moments I might reach out for a
bloody cross, an overflowing chalice, or the flaming
grail, whether they are there or not.

You know, hedging my bets, after a lifelong battle with
apparitions and illusions.

II

If I can still rise up a bit off my bed, I'll peek through
the drapes, like Phillip Marlowe on an all-night stakeout,
to see if the cabriolet and my driver are still there waiting
in the rain.

If it's way after dark, on a clear cold night I'll peek out
that big window to check the alignment of the bazillion
stars, planets and satellites, swirling around the heavens
above me.

III

There still might be a chance for me to fall in love with
my nurse or candy striper, both sweet muses in clean
uniforms, always so helpful with a smile and a catheter.

They come to say fare-thee-well every day, at least until
our next scheduled appointment, about dawn when I'm
finally getting to sleep.

One day they'll push my gurney down towards those huge
bronze doors at the end of the long hall, the most fun
I've had in years.

I'll be on my way, guided by experts in the dark,
making my last greasy fingerprints on the world's walls
as they push me along.

Hobo Bob Hummed This One

Stop your train, let a poor boy ride.
~Chester Burnett (Howlin' Wolf), *Smokestack Lightnin'*

Hobo Bob hummed this one to me once, at our
favorite roadhouse on the other side of the tracks.
He scribbled down the lyrics for me on some handy bar napkins.

I hum it now as I walk that way, down to the station
to catch that mystery train.

I sing it now as I walk that way, down to the station
to catch that mystery train.

A ticket I ain't got, as I watch it leave. A ticket I ain't got,
No, Sir, so I wave bye-bye. I don't ride this one, much
as I try.

One day I might, one day I might. One day I might,
I might, I might.

It'll be a fine day when the Conductor says hop on up, boy.

It will be that glory day when Mr. Conductor says you
hop on up, boy.

It will be that blessed day when Mr. Conductor says
hop on up, boy, this car is headin' towards joy.

It will be a very fine day when Mr. Conductor says hop
on up, boy, your silver train is headin' towards joy.

One day I might, one day I might. One day I might,
I might, I might.

But till then, I'll be waitin' down here, every mornin',
sweatin' in the shade, cryin' out to the big dust-mote
in the sky.

I'll be wonderin', yeah, wonderin' when my mystery train
will come back around, and it will be my turn, be my turn.

Dedicated to Me, Sez Hobo Bob

I
I scrawl this reminder from my empty grave
of resentment, only for the you that is me,

the author of my ills and blessings, each and every one,
even at my fifth birthday party out at the Lake.

Finally, I've quit blaming everyone. Certainly there
is plenty of blame to go round and round.

Perhaps, after all, it was a simple cognitive misattribution,
a linguistic *faux pas,* learned early from teachers galore.

I was only a child, so what did I know? I was taught
that things have these names,

when actually the thing was not the name that I had
so proudly learned.

Yeah, the name was not the thing. It was a trick and
something else entirely.

Of course, I've lived with these repercussions my entire
incredible life and I'm still tryin' to cry them all away.

II
I'm now turning it over, transmuting all those names,
all that blame, its adjacent rage and anger into thanks,
into forgiveness.

And, dare I say it, love.

To all those former blamees, you know who you may have
been. I'm now giving you all the credit for my genius, for
my vision, and to thank all of you profusely for your efforts,

for either encouraging me gently along my way, with a smile
and a kiss, or kicking me down the basement stairs
to break my heart and my spirit, just like at school.

So finally the world can leak in, and one day, maybe, poetry
can leak out.

III
We can spend our entire life carrying around buckets
overflowing with tearful blame, our *realous jage,*
because we think we must, that it is our fate.

Then one special day we decide to finally empty those angry
buckets back into the turbulent sea whence everything comes.

So for now, I'm beginning again. More cells, I grow more
cells daily to replace those that have died and sloughed off
in the night, mostly into my formerly tear-soaked pillow.

My new ones are now blameless and fresh and young.

Steven H. Bridgens

Born: August 17, 1949
Kansas City, Missouri

Died: January 31, 2017
Kansas City, Kansas

Resurrected that very same day, in fine shape after all

Current Fascinations: words, poems made of words, paintings,
assemblage, the rearrangement of the Ten Thousand Things,
sculpture & the mystery of the empty plinth, the ancient
world or the idea of it, silence & its absence, sleep & the
same, dead bluesmen & women, the artist & the muse, dead

gods & the demimonde, the primeval forest of Buddhism in its humble glory, the savage tyranny of the political stage, the toxic & enlightening proscenium of the internet, the Jungian depths of the self & the unconscious, the flickering shadows of cinema & architecture, the utopian possibilities of life on Garden Earth with our fellow passengers, all beings finally liberated.

This project was made possible, in part, by generous support from the Osage Arts Community.

Osage Arts Community provides temporary time, space and support for the creation of new artistic works in a retreat format, serving creative people of all kinds — visual artists, composers, poets, fiction and nonfiction writers. Located on a 152-acre farm in an isolated rural mountainside setting in Central Missouri and bordered by ¾ of a mile of the Gasconade River, OAC provides residencies to those working alone, as well as welcoming collaborative teams, offering living space and workspace in a country environment to emerging and mid-career artists. For more information, visit us at www.osageac.org